THIS BOOK BELONGS TO:

WELCOME TO VERMONT

Dedicated to all the explorers.

ISBN 978-1-958985-82-3

www.joeysavestheday.com

A Mimi Book

The name Vermont comes from the French words verts monts, which mean "green mountains."

France

Vermont was the fourteenth state to join the Union.
It officially joined on March 4, 1791.

14th

Vermont is located in the Northeastern region of the United States and is bordered by three states: New Hampshire, Massachusetts, and New York. Additionally, Vermont shares a northern border with Canada.

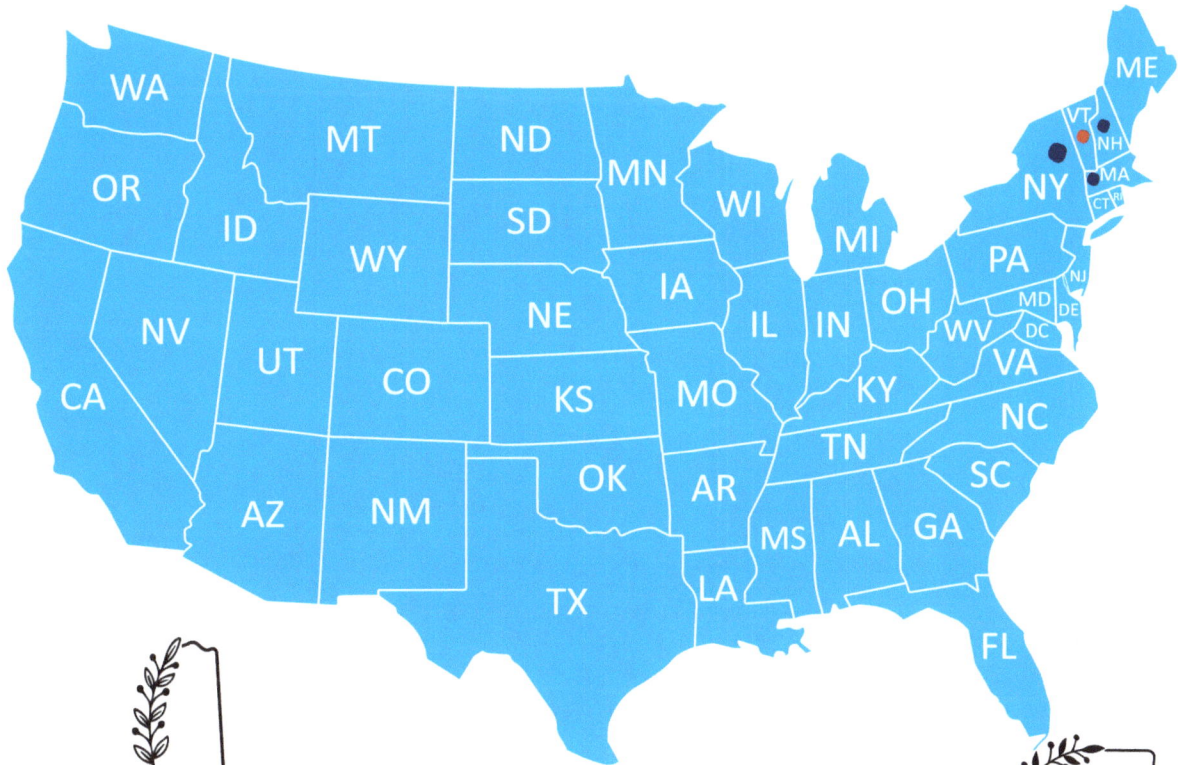

New Hampshire

Massachusetts

New York

Montpelier, Vermont, has an estimated population of about 8,000 people.

Vermont is the forty-fifth largest state in the United States by area, making it one of the smaller states in the country.

There are approximately 647,063 people residing in the state of Vermont.

Stowe, Vermont

John Deere was born in Rutland, Vermont, on February 7, 1804. He trained to become a blacksmith and after moving west, he invented the first successful steel plow. His idea grew into Deere & Company, a famous maker of tractors and farm machines.

Vermont is famous for making delicious maple syrup and produces more than any other U.S. state! Every spring the maple trees are tapped, and the sap is collected and boiled into the tasty syrup.

Vermont

There are 14 counties in Vermont.

Here is a list of those counties:

Addison	Franklin	Rutland
Bennington	Grand Isle	Washington
Caledonia	Lamoille	Windham
Chittenden	Orange	Windsor
Essex	Orleans	

Tunbridge, Vermont is a small, rural town known for its beautiful countryside and strong farming traditions. It is especially famous for the Tunbridge World's Fair, one of the oldest agricultural fairs in Vermont, where people come to see farm animals, crafts, and classic fair rides.

ONE DOLLAR FINE
FOR A PERSON TO DRIVE A HORSE
OR OTHER BEAST FASTER THAN
A WALK OR DRIVE MORE THAN ONE
LOADED TEAM AT THE SAME TIME
ON THIS BRIDGE

MILL BRIDGE 1883

15

Lake Iroquois is a small peaceful lake in Vermont that is popular for swimming, kayaking, and fishing. It is surrounded by forests and wildlife which makes it a great place to explore nature.

The historic Cooley Covered Bridge in Vermont is a wooden bridge that was built in 1849 to help people and wagons cross a river.

COOLEY BRIDGE
BUILT 1849

10'-9"

ONE LANE BRIDGE

SPEED LIMIT 15

17

Church Street in Burlington, Vermont, is a lively and colorful place where people love to gather. It is a special street called Church Street Marketplace, and it is closed to cars so people are able to walk freely to the various shops, restaurants and cafes lining the street.

The Vermont state bird is the Hermit Thrush. It was chosen as the state bird in 1941.

The official state flower of Vermont is the red clover. It was chosen as the state flower in 1895.

VERMONT

Vermont holds the distinction of having just one official state nickname: the Green Mountain State.

- the -

STATE

21

The state motto, "Freedom and Unity," has deep historical significance and was adopted in 1788, reflecting the values of the state and its people.

FREEDOM

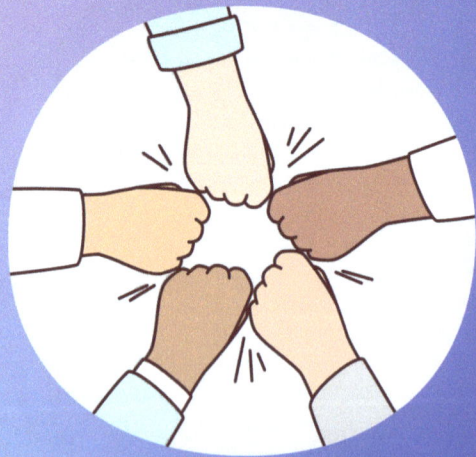

AND

VERMONT
VERMONT
VERMONT
VERMONT

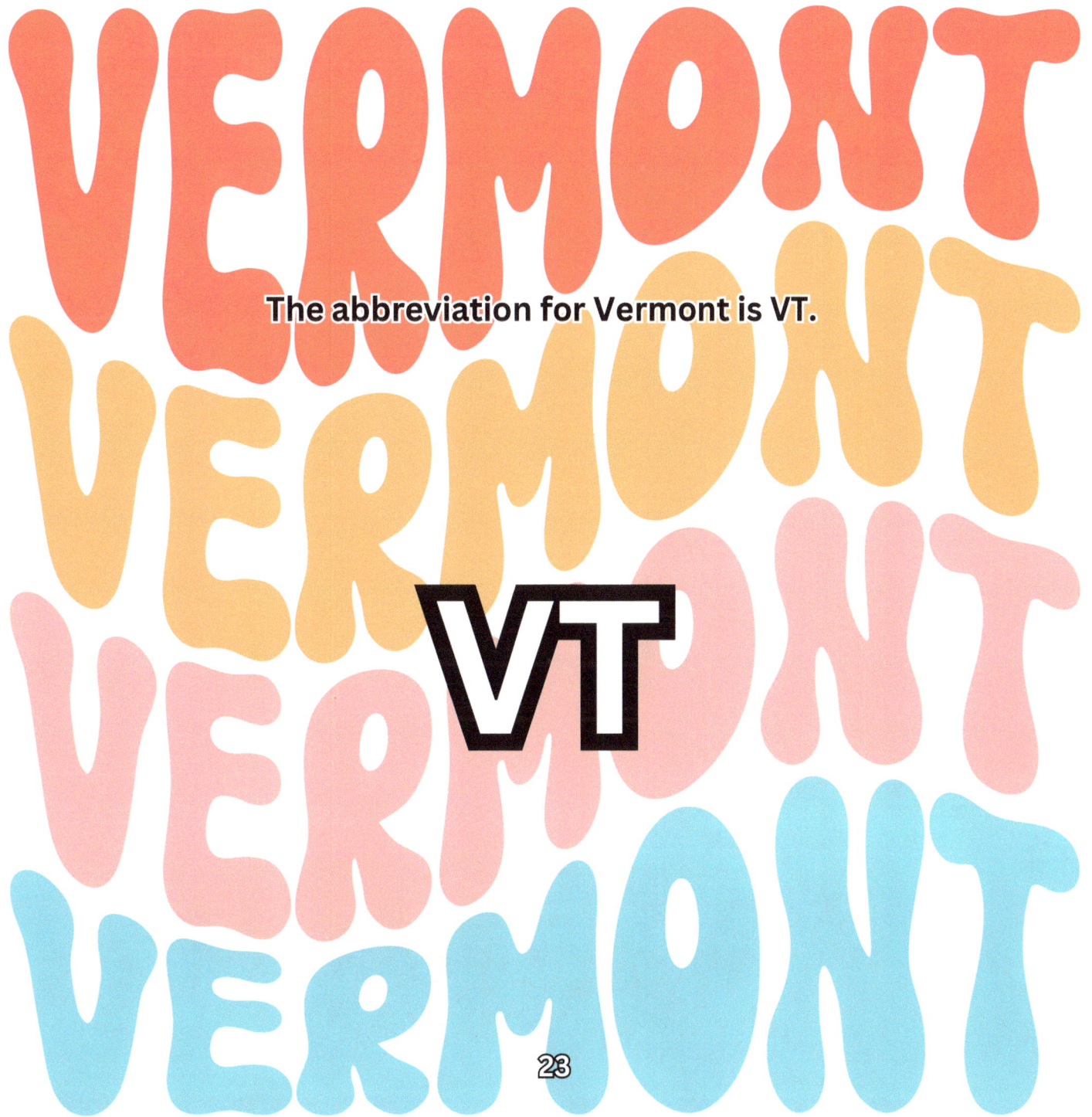

The abbreviation for Vermont is VT.

VT

The present state flag of Vermont was officially adopted on June 1, 1923.

Some crops grown in Vermont are apples, cherries, sweet potatoes, and zucchini.

Some animals that live in Vermont are black bears, beavers, chipmunks, squirrels, and rabbits.

Vermont exhibits considerable temperature fluctuations throughout the year. The highest temperature recorded in the state reached 105 degrees Fahrenheit in St. Johnsbury on July 4, 1911. In contrast, the lowest temperature, which was -50 degrees Fahrenheit (50 degrees below zero), occurred in Bloomfield on December 30, 1933.

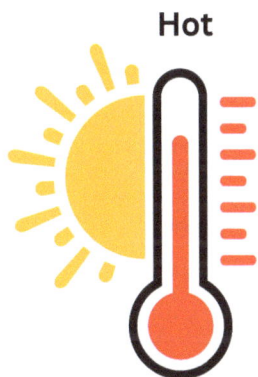

Hot

Cold

ZOO

The Vermont Institute of Natural Science, or VINS, is located in the small village of Quechee. Instead of a traditional zoo, it's a special nature center that cares for injured birds and teaches families about Vermont's wildlife. Kids can see bald eagles, owls, hawks, and other rescued birds up close, along with turtles, snakes, and small forest animals.

28

The Montshire Museum of Science located in Norwich, Vermont, is a hands-on science museum. It's a place where kids can touch, build, explore, and experiment. Inside are fun exhibits about light, sound, bubbles, weather, space, and nature.

The Burlington International Airport, located in South Burlington, Vermont, is the state's busiest airport and a major gateway for travelers visiting the Green Mountains. It's only a few minutes from downtown Burlington and close to beautiful Lake Champlain.

The Vermont Lake Monsters are a summer baseball team based in Burlington, Vermont. They play their home games at Centennial Field, one of the oldest ballparks in the country. The team brings big energy, teamwork, and a splash of friendly monster fun to every game.

31

FOOTBALL

The Vermont Catamounts are a spirited football team based in Burlington, Vermont, where students and fans cheer them on with Green Mountain pride. They play their home games on campus, bringing energy, teamwork, and Vermont spirit to every matchup. The Catamounts' colors are green and gold to celebrate the forests and fall leaves that make Vermont famous. Their fierce catamount mascot honors the wild, adventurous spirit that has shaped Vermont's history.

The Sugar Maple is Vermont's state tree, chosen in 1949. It's loved for its bright fall colors and for the sweet sap that becomes maple syrup. These tall, sturdy trees help make Vermont's forests beautiful and its maple season delicious.

33

Vermont has two official state fish: the Brook Trout and the Walleye. The Brook Trout lives in Vermont's cold, clear mountain streams and is known for its bright spots and colorful belly. The Walleye prefers the state's deeper lakes and is famous for its shiny eyes and strong swimming.

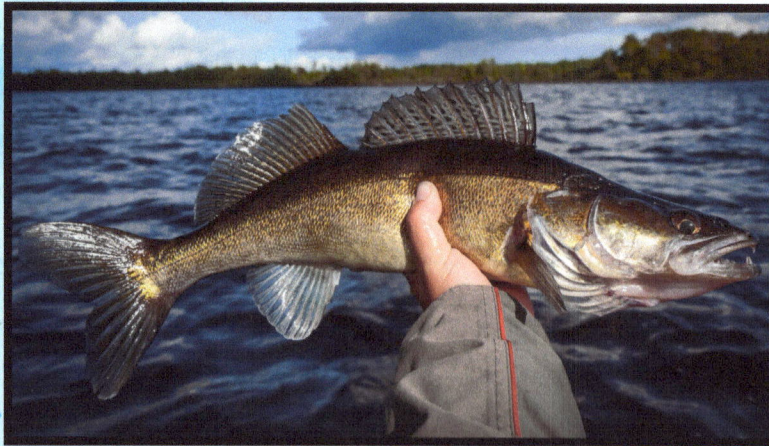

Can you name these?

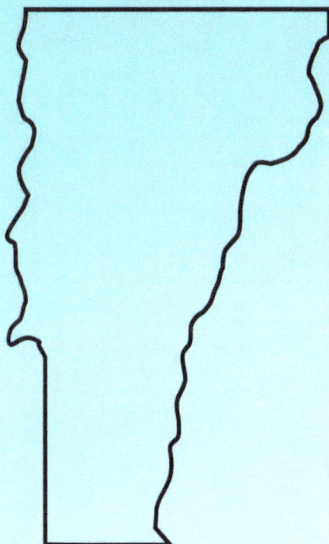

I hope you enjoyed learning about Vermont.

To explore fun facts about the other 49 states, visit my website at www.joeysavestheday.com. You'll also find a wide variety of homeschool resources to support joyful learning at home. If you enjoyed this book, I would be grateful if you left a review. Your feedback truly helps. Thank you for your support!

TIME TO SAY GOODBYE

Check out these other interesting books in the 50 States Fact Books Series!

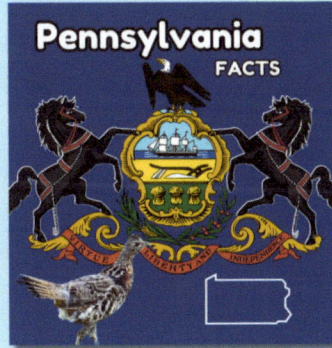

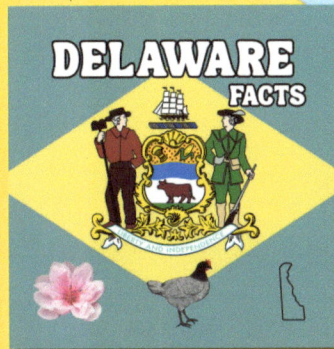

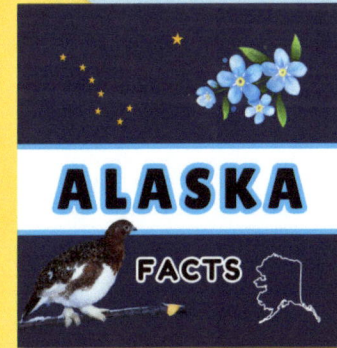

OHIO FACTS

Pennsylvania FACTS

TEXAS FACTS

DELAWARE FACTS

CALIFORNIA FACTS

KENTUCKY FACTS

COMMONWEALTH OF KENTUCKY
UNITED WE STAND
DIVIDED WE FALL

GEORGIA FACTS

ALABAMA Facts

ALASKA FACTS

www.mimibooks.com

www.ingramcontent.com/pod-product-compliance
Lightning Source LLC
Chambersburg PA
CBHW041549040426

42447CB00002B/112

* 9 7 8 1 9 5 8 9 8 5 8 2 3 *